A BABY'S LITTLE INSTRUCTION BOOK

A BABY'S LITTLE
INSTRUCTION BOOK

David Brawn

Thorsons
An Imprint of HarperCollins*Publishers*

Thorsons
An Imprint of HarperCollins*Publishers*
77–85 Fulham Palace Road,
Hammersmith, London W6 8JB

Published by Thorsons 1995
1 3 5 7 9 10 8 6 4 2

David Brawn asserts the moral right to
be identified as the author of this work

Illustrations by Mike Gordon

A catalogue record for this book
is available from the British Library

ISBN 0 7225 3103 6

Printed in Great Britain by
HarperCollinsManufacturing Glasgow

To Sarah and Georgia
for such marvellous inspiration

And to their mummy, Tracey,
who did most of the research

INTRODUCTION

WE all start our passage through life as babies. Like it or not, we've all been there, and when we come to have children ourselves, we encounter the same frustrations and make the same mistakes as all other parents, including our own. If a baby were writing his or her own manual, describing how best to embarrass or try the patience of the most switched-on parent, this is the book that would result. The

300 or so instructions are just a few of the inevitable infuriations babies cause as they learn the boundaries of social behaviour and push their parents near the ends of tethers they had no idea could be so long. The book *may* serve as preparation for the unsuspecting new parent, but is probably no more practical than any affectionate tribute to the ingenuity and inventiveness of those who shall inherit our future. Thank goodness they all – eventually – grow up!

And just what *is* a baby? As far as *A Baby's Little Instruction Book* goes, if it covered only the first six months of life, it would likely contain just four instructions, detailing the processes of sleeping, crying, eating and filling one's nappy (or diaper, if you prefer). I have therefore chosen to include the early toddling years, up to about three and a half, when most children are canny enough to have become mini-adults in their own right – they certainly expect to be treated as such. The instructions themselves are not arranged in any particular order – babies develop at different rates, and some will talk before they can walk, or draw on the wallpaper before they embark on potty training, or cut their first teeth before they sleep through the night. To try and impose a progressive order in the book would therefore be quite impossible. Suffice it to say, for those readers with babies and young children of their own, if you are not yet familiar with any of the items of behaviour mentioned, rest assured your little cherub will be doing these very soon!

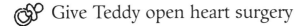 Give Teddy open heart surgery

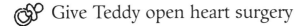 Insist on being breastfed until after you've cut your first teeth

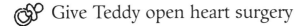 Drink from fish bowls

Wipe sticky hands on a visitor's dress

Demolish shop window displays

If you find a tiny hole in a jumper, pull at it until it's no longer a tiny hole

Don't waste a good drink – only ever spill one if you know it will stain

Demand to watch the same video over and over and over again

Scream in the supermarket

Always embarrass an older brother or sister among schoolfriends

Call the childminder 'Mummy' in front of your own mother

Always find an excuse not to go clothes shopping

Use the toilet on display in a DIY store

Remember that 'Don't touch' is a licence to handle things

Suckle on anything vaguely nipple-shaped

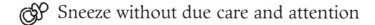 Sneeze without due care and attention

Suck the label

Insist on your own ice cream cone – not just a lick of someone else's

Refuse to eat your dinner, yet have room for dessert

Develop a special cry for real emergencies

Carry a newborn brother or sister when no one is looking

Develop rashes that look far worse than they are

Never believe an adult who tells you a plate, teapot or radiator is hot – insist on investigating for yourself, then crying as though it's *their* fault

Jam your baby walker behind the door

Learn to open child safety locks

Leave sticky handprints on photographs

Dribble in other people's drinks

Block the toilet with laundry

Prefer a cassette to mummy reading a story

Turn off the television when they're watching the news

Push the stop button on escalators

 Learn to tell realistic tales

Be an angel at the childminder's and a monster at home

Embarrass your parents at every opportunity

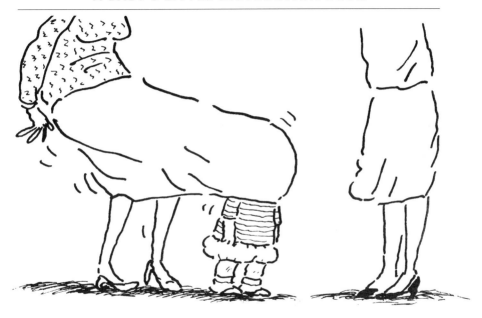

Don't let Mummy use you as an excuse to queue-jump at the Ladies

Experiment with your mother's make-up bag

Change the rules to suit yourself

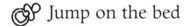 Jump on the bed

Burst your balloon and then believe the world
has come to an end

Only choose breakfast cereal by virtue of the
free gift

Do not allow your pram to be used as a substitute shopping trolley

Refuse to take your medicine

Be able to identify medicine even if 'disguised' in food or drink

Throw toys out of your pram and have people go back to look for them

Impress Granny with your new tricks

Never go out without your comforter

Never allow your dirtiest soft toy to be washed

Crayon in story books

Go organic — eat mud

Start a collection of sharp objects

Play with peas on your plate – don't under any circumstance *eat* them

Stick marbles up your nose

Tear covers off magazines

 Play with wrapping paper and ignore the presents

Ask for your potty *after* the event

Invent new names for things and insist on using them until the whole family is doing it

Learn to feign injury

Pull at loose joins in the wallpaper

Never be seen in clothes handed down from a child of the opposite sex

Don't speak if pointing will do

Learn to distinguish between the sexes

Pick up bad language from your parents quicker than any other words

If you're going to lie, do it convincingly

Hate having your hair washed

Tell people you're an orphan for sympathy

Blow bubbles — eat soap

Only poo in the bath if you're sharing it with a parent

Throw up in the car without giving warning

Be unable to blow your nose properly

Have your parents take you out for a walk in the night to get you back to sleep

Call your maternal grandmother to her face by the name your father uses when she's not there

Pick your nose

Empty waste paper bins

Don't let your mother raid your money box to pay the milkman

Don't admit to missing your parents when they leave you at a relative's for the night

Insist on junk food in preference to healthy alternatives

Prove that no nappy is leak-proof

Never take 'No' for an answer

Always wipe your mouth after being kissed by an elderly relative

Train your parents, but let them think they're training you

Don't sit still when having your hair cut

Fall out of bed without waking up

Be reluctant to share your toys with other children

Enjoy repetitive musical toys that grate on adults' nerves

Be afraid of Father Christmas

Talk all the way through your first visit to the cinema

Be ticklish

Induce heart attacks – stand up in your high-chair

When learning to stand up, ensure you know how to sit down again

Perfect the art of moving around only when you're on your own

Sleep in the same bed as your parents when:
a) You have nightmares
b) You're poorly
c) You know they want to try and expand the family!

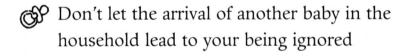 Don't let the arrival of another baby in the household lead to your being ignored

Refuse to eat the meals that have taken the longest to prepare

Ensure your first ever homemade Christmas decorations are displayed prominently, no matter how amateurish they look

Be ashamed of your parents

Don't eat chips without ketchup

Don't eat anything without chips

Fill your nappy immediately it's been changed

Sneeze with your mouth full

Poke at people's eyes

Ensure your parents never have the time to get up to anything

Demand attention during *Coronation Street*

Never be tempted to pull at fake jewellery – only the real thing

Suck your thumb

Play with coal

Insist on being rocked to sleep, no matter how long it takes

Ensure more dinner goes in your hair than your mouth

Burst other toddlers' balloons

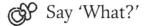 Say 'What?'

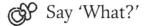 Show your underwear to strangers

 Be able to retrieve a small morsel of vegetable out of a mouthful of food

Suck your top lip until your nose stops running

Learn to say 'No' before you learn to say 'Yes'

Insist on having as many lights on as possible at night

Fall asleep in Mummy's bed, but threaten to wake up when being transferred back to your cot, so you can stay in the warm

Wear your shoes on the wrong feet

Exhibit irrational terror at the sight of a uniform

No matter how long it takes, never stop crying until they give in

Wee in the swimming pool

Don't drink the water in the swimming pool

Stare at people in the changing room

Attempt to breastfeed from anybody who picks you up

Get your legs stuck between the bars of your cot

Say 'please' – it is the quickest route to getting your own way

Fake serious illness, and recover in the time it takes to get to the doctor's

Throw up on clean clothes

Lose your bootees when you're out

Put sweets in the shopping trolley which won't be noticed until after they've been paid for

Never be seen in a frilly sunhat

Eat out of your bib in preference to your bowl

Be adventurous with your food – worms, woodlice, snails, but *never* greens

Answer the telephone before anyone can get to it

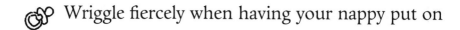 Wriggle fiercely when having your nappy put on

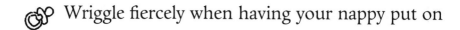 When being changed, stick your feet in the dirty nappy before it's been taken off the changing mat

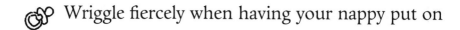 Develop a squint

Never stay pristine for very long

Avoid having a dirty face 'cleaned' with a grown up's tissue covered in spit!

Climb on the furniture, especially at other people's houses

Press your face up against shop windows

Leave handprints on mirrors

Eat off other people's plates, but not your own

Have a favourite plaything that isn't a toy

Remember, if God had intended you to use cutlery, he'd have given you metal fingers

Drop your dummy in the font at your Christening

Play with fragile ornaments

Talk to strangers

Don't let bribery lead you to give up something you really want

Learn how to play one parent off against the other

Be selectively deaf when being called

Demand that baby wipes are warmed before application

Never keep a secret

Open other people's presents

Insist on an expensive novelty toothbrush

Hide the television remote controller

Pull the tape out of cassettes

⊗ Don't drink from a cup in place of a bottle

⊗ Tell your grandparents they're wrinkly

⊗ Pull off toupées

⊗ Skid around on your potty

Empty visitors' handbags

Demand coins from strangers

Jump in puddles in unsuitable footwear

Eat play dough

Never walk when you can ride in the pushchair

Eat out of the cat's dish

Learn how to 'accidentally' telephone the emergency services

Pull heads off flowers

Get plenty of sleep during the day so you are at your wakeful best throughout the night

Have temper tantrums over trivial matters in very public places

Pull the cat's tail

Bite hard when someone's feeling your new teeth

Don't trust a man with a beard

In a room full of people, always make a beeline for the one who hates children

Always wee during a nappy change

Give the dog a haircut

Manage to reach things even when they're supposed to be out of reach

Don't let your parents get away with imposing a sweetie-free diet

Never take the blame for anything

Pull ugly faces when being photographed for a cute baby competition

Never show any intelligence during formal assessments

Make rude noises from every orifice, and smile

If you build a snowman, don't plan a long-term relationship with him

Don't be afraid to learn traditional rhymes, and boycott any 'politically correct' versions

Play with toys that promote sexual stereotypes – of the opposite persuasion!

Walk in the gutter

If you go anywhere particularly 'grown up', endeavour to be especially naughty

Insist on 'having a word' on every telephone conversation

Ask you parents what sex is at an unreasonably young age – they won't be expecting the question

Talk with your mouth full

Have a box of tissues ready for the ritual kissing goodbye

Crayon on the wallpaper in preference to writing paper

Tell tales

Be friendly towards total strangers yet scream hysterically at close relatives

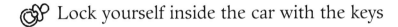 Lock yourself inside the car with the keys

When potty training:
    a) Remember to pull your pants down
    b) Display your achievements to all and sundry
    c) Don't wee over the edge

Don't have such a silly name for your private parts that people don't know what you're telling them about

When sleeping in Mummy's bedroom, snuffle and wheeze so she can't sleep

Never call the milkman 'Dad' (unless he is)

Dance to *Top of the Pops*

Know where the biscuits are kept and when they have not, in fact, 'all gone'

Learn to count from 1 to 10, but not necessarily in that order

Say 'Sorry' when you've been naughty (even if you're not)

Pester to be taken out to play when Mummy's got a hangover

Always discover contraceptives, no matter how well hidden, and ask what they are

Show your inquisitiveness by taking your auntie something she's really afraid of, like a spider

Scream at your Christening, even before you get to the bit with the water

Expect to be fed on demand – just like Daddy

Instil a sense of parental guilt by yelling at your inoculations, even if you can't feel a thing

Get your fingers caught in the holes in your blanket

Learn to pull out electrical socket covers

When putting trousers on, only lift your left foot *after* you've put your right foot back on the floor – or you'll fall over

Blaspheme, just as Daddy does, at Playgroup

Disfigure your favourite teddy bear with too much love

Establish your own sleeping routine

Give your soft toys really imaginative names, like 'Dog', 'Rabbit' and 'Mouse'

Bruise yourself in time for the appointment with the health visitor

Shut your fingers in cupboard doors

Grab the spoon when being fed

Run out of the lift when the doors are closing

Train an older sibling to be your unpaid slave

 Bite fruit in the greengrocer's and put it back

Three ways to wipe your nose without a tissue:
a) On your sleeve
b) On someone else's jumper
c) With your tongue

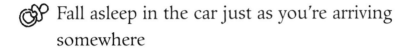 Fall asleep in the car just as you're arriving somewhere

Climb over the stairgate

Get your head stuck in your playpen

Go rigid when you don't want to sit in your pushchair

Make sure your early paintings are treated with respect

Blow bubbles in your drink

Lock yourself in the toilet

Lock someone else in the toilet

Ruin 'quality time'

Cultivate a dirty laugh

Lift your dress in public

Lift Mummy's dress in public

Practise emotional blackmail – try 'Nobody loves me' when you're being ignored

Make nuisance phone calls

Pull faces when having a family photograph taken

Share your breakfast with the dog

Pull your socks off at every opportunity

Be unsociable towards Mummy's friends' children

Bang on the table

In a toyshop, never settle for least expensive

In a sweetshop, never settle for a small packet

In a clothes shop, never settle for something tasteful

Never open your mouth for the dentist

Don't let Daddy bury you on a beach – it is inevitable that he will deliberately upset you by pretending to leave

Put your potty on your head

Blame your baby sister for your own misdemeanours

Demand to wear reins in department stores – just to slow Mummy down

Don't play with toys with an obvious 'educational' value

Stamp your feet when you can't get your own way

Always ask 'Why?', even if you know the answer

Walk in the gutter

- Fall down the stairs the day the stairgate is left open

- Giggle when you poop

- Giggle when someone else poops, especially if they think they got away with it

Don't come home from shopping without a toy or some sweets

If there's water about, fall in it

Pester for horrid toys you've seen advertised on television

Stare at people you don't know

Perform the 'choke' test by putting everything in your mouth

Pull a knot in your shoelaces that it is impossible for anyone for untie

Ask the baker for a gingerbread *person*

Make sure you get both Mum *and* Dad up at night

Manage to pull the safety eyes off your teddy

Persuade Daddy to stick a rubber suction cup on his forehead so it leaves a bruise

Rearrange Nana's ornaments

Learn which parent is the softest touch

Make disparaging comments about a friend's parents' car

Whine for a biscuit, then say you don't like any of the ones on offer

Smile and you'll get your own way

Bring new meaning to the phrase 'accident prone'

Teach the dog bad habits

Learn bad habits from the dog

Learn to project your vomit accurately

Dribble profusely when teething

Pull old ladies' hair on the bus or train

Unravel toilet rolls

Post the front door keys through the letterbox

Be computer literate by the time you're three

Fall asleep when someone's talking to you

Cut your own hair

Wipe muddy hands on your clothes

Never let parents forget a promise

Put both feet in the same trouser leg

Sneeze at talcum powder

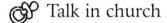 Talk in church

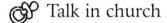 Always be the centre of attention

 Say your shoes hurt even if they don't, just so you'll get a new pair

🍼 Try out your new teeth, but not on yourself

🍼 Undo your own seatbelt

🍼 Spot the moral at the end of a cartoon

🍼 Scribble on important documents

Leave half sucked lollipops on the sofa

Leave toy cars on the stairs

Announce when you're going to the toilet, and describe your accomplishments when you return

Remember, your mummy loves you, even if everyone else thinks you're smelly, noisy, ugly and difficult

A DOG'S
LITTLE INSTRUCTION BOOK

- Don't drink from a bowl with CAT on it
- Keep your tail down when it's windy
- Make friends with the local butcher
- Never be seen in tartan
- Don't eat slug pellets (or slugs)
- Chase frisbees but not boomerangs
- When you get old, learn some new tricks

A TEDDY BEAR'S
LITTLE INSTRUCTION BOOK

• Never serve your porridge then go out for a walk

• Don't wear your duffle coat in the house

• If you're made of mohair, ponder on the nature of a mo

• Don't be part exchanged for a computer game

• Be brave – sleep with the light off

• Don't become a projectile in domestic disputes

• Follow fashion – don't be the bear behind